LATEST VOLCANO

TANA JEAN WELCH

MARSH

HAWK

PRESS

2016

FIRST EDITION 10 9 8 7 6 5 4 3 2 1

Marsh Hawk Press books are published by Poetry Mailing List, Inc., a not-for-profit
corporation under section 501 (c) 3 United States Internal Revenue Code.

Cover art: *Falling Teeth* by aleks bartosik, 2014. www.aleksbartosik.com
Used by permission. (Photographed by Lauretta Santarossa.)

Cover and interior design by Heather Wood. www.heatherwoodbooks.com
The text is set in Garamond Premier Pro.

Library of Congress Cataloging-in-Publication Data
Welch, Tana Jean.
[Poems. Selections]
Latest volcano / Tana Jean Welch. — First edition.
pages   cm
ISBN 978-0-9906669-8-1 (pbk.) — ISBN 0-9906669-8-0 (pbk.)
I. Title. PS3623.E4636A6 2016   811'.6—dc23   2015026415

Marsh Hawk Press
P.O. Box 206, East Rockaway, NY 11518-0206
www.marshhawkpress.org

FOR TIMOTHY

CONTENTS

III. Dragon-Dance

LATEST

VOLCANO

And we are left, as scorpions ringed with fire.
What should we do but strike ourselves to death?

—PERCY BYSSHE SHELLEY, *THE CENCI*

The Centaur's Daughter

How Much Poison?

She's collecting scorpions—
getting them before they get her. In the attic,

in the bathtub, she finds
the tiny toxic lobsters laced

between her bed sheets. Lets them loose
at the base of the lemon tree,

starts the game over. One by one
until the box is full. The scorpion

is her sigil. Her love song on the battlefield,
her war-cry in the senseless fields. Survive

on nothing, on one insect a year. Dagger
your tail, desert-dweller. Peel the bark,

hold it to your mother's throat,
ask her why there is no grave to visit,

nothing to tap and touch *hello, I miss you,*
not even an urn with your father's ashes.

She Took the Gun

She took the gun
and walked
to the reservoir behind the stitched line
of tract homes.

She always knew the pearl-handled revolver
was under her mother's bed,
could sometimes hear
it breathing
on the nights she couldn't sleep.

Stepping out of the shadows
of hackberry, red oak,
she arrived at the water's edge and found
no clouds in the reflection.
Blank sky, no shield,
nothing between her and the blue universe,
the loud sun, but
blood is never brightness

and today
there was blood on her underwear
for the first time
and the girl knew
she wouldn't tell her mother,
not now, maybe never. Because her mother
would say it was *something*

and the girl knew it was nothing,
felt like nothing,
just like the gun in her hand
wasn't heavy or cold.

Just like shooting into the water
felt like nothing

until
two fish rose to the surface,
mouths gaping open
like children singing in the midnight choir,
paper wings wired
to their backs, or like children
in a furnace, stomachs bloated
and empty.

Nothing To See Here

The girl takes a bus across town
to the Pan de Vida and buys
a rosary. On the return trip
she crimps the brown beads in her palm
and pretends she is a Catholic.

She imagines herself on pilgrimage to Cologne,
peering into the hearts of 11,000 virgins.

She wants to see the arsenal
of ribs, shoulder blades, and femurs—the riot
of relics resting in the basilica. Pray
to St. Ursula's martyred handmaids:

touch the skull caps of twenty virgins
say ten Hail Marys
and you get to start over—

her body unspoiled, her body
never pressed against damp dirt
in a wide field, bluestem grass waving
a secret fortress around bare skin.

She imagines a priest feeding her apple strudel,
wrapping her in red cloth.

She ponders the logistics of beheading 11,000 girls:
How many Huns did it take? How much blood,
how long?

What Remains

Bulls with bells around their necks, large black bulls
flipping over in dust, dancing with yards of yellow silk.

Her father carrying her through the gates of the arena,
an easel strapped to his back, a warm *churro* in her small fist.

Bulls slowly turning red at the bite of each lance. People outside
the arena, glazed red, shouting under buckets of insincere blood,

to make a point, her father said. People inside cheering, waving
white handkerchiefs, hoping to be thrown a tail or a hoof.

After his death, the girl spent months trying to believe in ghosts
who smelled like her father: Old Spice, Budweiser,

linseed—she managed to muster a phantom father dragging
his old brushes and paint over canvas, an exact likeness

who stayed in nightclothes till dinner, smashed empty beer cans—
But soon enough her mother sold the last painting

and the spirit sped away, popping wheelies
on a damaged motorcycle without saying so much as goodbye.

Slowly she forgot his voice and the shape
of his face until all that was left were the bulls.

The matador in the bull ring, real blood seeping from his stomach.
A single memory to live by: her father telling her it was good to see

both a bull pocked with the spears of the *picadores* and a matador
   gored,
the needle-sharp horn of the plowbeast piercing clean through.

Horse-Driven Men

the runaway:

I can use my body to straddle
or save the universe,

to be a soft animal
                        for a man
or woman who knows how to touch and

travel the surface of my quiet skin, how to span
                        the bridge—

it's all right to miss my mother and I do
                        when I see the lemon tree
in the courtyard, when I pick one to slice through

                I see sugar drops, but no ditch reeds,
        no scorpions in sight. Once I

    cried a thrum
            of tears.

I surveyed the stars,
like when dad died: our backs to the grass, sucking on rum
lifesavers, red vines, my mother and I gazing at the lost centaur

who succumbed
to a brilliant loss of control

and scattered his armor from pole to pole.

The Third Time She Ran Away

She found herself heading north toward Norine
whose internet photo reminded her of Lara Croft, Tomb Raider

but the long braid was a bluff, something that slips off
                    like a lizard's tail lost
                    to a rabid raccoon.

                  By then the girl was never used
to things being what they seemed. Like how
Norine's apartment was black as a coalhole
and cold as the bus depot in Fond du Lac
where Norine, in her "you'll know me when you see me"
                  orange scarf, first appeared—
                  a filigree angel in an '88 Camero,
                          T-roof open despite the drifting snow.
          It was a dark chill room, but to pull the thick drape
from the large window, to touch the afternoon light spreading
          over Norine's Craigslisted body
          asleep on the bed—

                  the girl traced the hiss
        of the orange scarf around
Norine's legs, remembered Norine's tongue
pawing along her thighs, Norine's larger, fuller breasts
pressing against her own—
she might be good for something after all

and turned to the city
below—cleaner, taller than El Paso—pressed her nipples
against the glass pane, letting the drape fall behind her:

A child hiding between worlds, she watched a man
walking an orange Abyssinian on a leash
     and remembered someone singing
          Harry Chapin at her father's funeral.

There was a cat yesterday:
              A lion locked behind plexiglass,
         Norine and the girl walking through
        the Field Museum, the orange scarf draped
          over their shoulders, stopping
   to stare at the man-eater, to imagine themselves
filled with his teeth. The lion of Mfuwe murdered six
     then paraded through the Zambian village with a haversack
       full of the last dead man's clothes.

The Same Wide Feet

the runaway's mother:

I spent my life teaching her about men
and poison, making sure she knew a woman must behave
as a turtle: learn what to hide, what to show:

rest nothing on the nightstand except mango and shea,
a candle, an alarm clock   an electric glow
an invitation   a long but high slit dress   censor

then uncensor   because what's inside matters most:
an exhausted copy of Thucydides' *History*   the usual lace
and underwire veiling the bottle of Astroglide, the pot of blackberry

jelly—a strong woman, like Cleopatra, heaves through
the senators' snares   then unfurls her body
on the soft spun-cotton sheets   cataclastic   guilty

in living   and loving the politics of her own orgasm.

When my daughter left for the last time   she returned
the suede miniskirt, the red heels   her little, undressed
frame   in the dim light   formed its final claim:

The power that lies in the body is no power at all.

I lent her my mascara, my shadow—not every daughter wants
to feed on the leather of her mother's loneliness. This one forged
a crust over her heart, then sat safely   watching mine burn to dust.

While Waiting

while waiting for a herd of bighorn sheep
to cross Highway 34, she spread
the park brochure across the steering wheel

there were facts like everything else even sheep
had facts   ewes and rams
live in separate herds

ewes are smaller but live longer

sex in November but only after
an elaborate ramming of ram against ram

like the ranger pressing against her car door
Am I dead, Angel? Cause this must be heaven!

the hoofs soft and flexible
the stomach in four parts

both male and female sheep have true horns

black bears are not always black

and the white rump of the last sheep crossing in front of her car:
like the cotton spilling
out of her teddy bear
as she cut off its head with pruning shears:
finding the white stuff
rough to the touch, not at all soft

The Dragon-Dance

—to the runaway, the centaur's daughter

You find yourself in Calgary
paying Sister Fay two dollars to look at the lines
      in your palm, translate the creases
            into a vision of Chinatown: *two streets*

north and five south, go find the water-carrier.
And she can't tell you anything more because two dollars
      only gets you so much, and because this is your journey,
            your long-trembling path, and what else

did you expect? Inside the shell, the book,
the boarding house room—aren't you always finding the echo
      of everything else? And the echo says Chinatown
            so you walk the Centre Street Bridge

over the snow-banks of the Bow River,
wearing the jacket and boots given by your last lover,
      the one who left you alone at Lake Louise, left you
            singing to the snowmen and the fir tree spires,

a lonely lunatic taking pictures
of ice castles and children. But there is no time to think
      about this or the water-carrier. The bridge ends—
            feeding you into a brighter night,

into a lake of red paper lanterns, a field
of fiery pomegranates hanging in the cold Canadian sky,
    glowing like Plath's pink fever moons—
        a canopy covering a throng of people.

Frosty breath gleaming amid firecracker spark,
you overhear someone say: *a beautiful woman lives on the moon*
    making medicine, and someone ask for yuanxiao
        with rose petals, and someone tell

the story of a girl who jumped into a well,
and someone whisper *the Jade Emperor lost his favorite crane*,
    and someone else say *this Lantern Festival is smaller*
        but better than Toronto's—

and it isn't hard to make these stories
meaningful and applicable to your own life because
    you are hungry and the smell of smoke and honey
        is a persistent worm winding

through your nose, like the dragon
spinning toward you, its one-hundred human legs running,
    the golden body an eternal corkscrew, a cloud cave—
        until you realize you are in its path,

the whirlpool, the chomping legs:
after all these state-lines and all these years, seeking the darkness
    of strangers, biting your own tail, spitting, spitting,
        your destiny becomes clear:

carry the dragon as it carries you,
find the thick pearl lodged in your throat, close your eyes,
wait to see if the Canadians will push you free,
if you'll feel the pull

of your arm, body sucked into the gyre.
If, inside the dragon, your hands will grip a long bamboo pole
as a man lifts, dips and thrusts his body
against yours, moving

effortlessly on its own, fluidly,
as easy as filling a glass of water beneath a faucet
or a fountain, a wellspring. If his hand will press
your hand into the bamboo

and feel exactly like someone who carries
the genius of thunder, the safety of hand-made quilts, exactly
like someone who would never leave you
alone at Lake Louise.

If Like a Crab

she could go backward
to the barnacles on the legs
of the pier, a family crabbing
in the shallows of Savannah,
Tybee Island in the distance,
and the lighthouse
where the winds blew
her mother's white hat into the Atlantic,
long hair let loose and whipping
     like a sheet of brown silk
        or a flag
            erasing her face
    for a moment
until a rubber band anchored the strands—
a maritime knot,
    a monkey's fist—

They lived in a van then.
Moving under thunderheads, stars,
in tune with the constellations
to Blue Ridge Mountains, Pennsylvania Dutch, old French
in Quebec. Her father believed in constant
                    motion.

Stay still and love
fades. So they drove, fleeting
    like Halley's Comet, the naked-eye
worm-coil engine   stopping only once
a lifetime.

And now, after spending half her life
drifting rivulet to river, blaming her mother
           for her father's death, she knew
           she could never go back.

She thought she'd been flying—volatile,
a celestial body, her father's daughter
         from Chicago to New York to Calgary—
            her movement had never been anything

but lateral and alongside her mother's white hat blowing
        across tall grasses, kissing the head
           of the lone heron before sailing

        into the discontented waves of the Eastern sea.

She could never go back
to her father tying turkey necks to strings,
her father who always   tossed back the lady crabs,
            their painted red claws,
first daring her to touch one
        while it clamped in the dip net.

Seven Things She Learned Along the Way

1.
Complete dead sound is difficult to balance.
She walks in soft moccasins, matching
the cadence of the one she follows—
she steps safely over every trip wire,
but can still hear the blue heron
getting bluer. Still hear the pulse of the solitary bark beetle.

2.
It's hard to steady her body under the influence
of opposing forces. Against the landlord's naked son in SoHo.
Against strong men in carpet caps. Like Theodora tagging
the side of a building while on MJ and codeine.
Theodora's sister flaunting their shared seven minutes
of heaven. She could never stand tall when taunted
by a bare breast. Even if it made Theodora cry.
Even if the closet was dark.

3.
Under certain circumstances the tale acts as a balance.
When her father died, she told herself he'd gone abroad,
painting for tourists on the banks of the Seine.
He'll send for you soon. When the sheriff raped her,
she told herself he was a prince
turned into a nightingale turned into a dragon
who could only return to his former self
by breaking down her thatched hut, by ripping her into a doll.

4.

Keep steady, at all times, one leg over the balcony-rail.
In case she needs a different city. In case she wants
to touch the moon or the apricots hanging over the gates.
Because you never know what the letter says until you slit
open the envelope. You'll want the luxury of flexibility
in case the words typed in blue   tangle together,
fall   and pile into an unhappy mess
on the motel bedspread. In case she wants
to come back.   In case she needs someone else.

5.

*The attraction of the glass is balanced by the contrary
attraction of the liquor.* The attraction of the water
surrounding the colonial bridge, the Dutch reeds. Green glass.
Her face in his hands. Her hands throwing the bottle
against his bare knees. Distill: to drip, to wet, to drop
her essence in every paper bag across the country, kinetic
energy plus particle attraction: safety in numbers. Part
of me will meet you in Concord. But only part.

6.

So many things balance the sorrow of it.
The pearls of a pomegranate. Timothy
in the afternoon. Gargoyles hanging on ancient eaves.
Fête de la Nouvelle-France in Quebec City.
Verbena. Sea-cliff mountain fragments.
The ocean rolling us all to sleep.

7.
She learned *to oscillate like the beam of a balance.*
To swing backwards and forwards. To move
between two points. To vibrate and remember:
It's not safety in numbers, but safety in movement.
To be vibrant, like the tiger butterfly
migrating during monsoon season. Tell yourself:
You are the Nazca astronaut. You are
the latest volcano, not the latest eruption.

The Last Years of the Napoleonic Wars

Now the constant traveler is in Brussels,
walking round the Lion's Mound near Waterloo,
thinking about the history of tourism—
tour derived from *tornus*, Latin for the turner's lathe,
a wheel, a tool for shaping circular bodies:
bowls and baseball bats, columns and pillars.
She learns the mound is a monument
marking where the prince was merely wounded.
He lived thirty more years, long enough
to smell the flowers grown from the bones
of the 50,000 battle-dead men—
bones dug up and sent to Yorkshire a few years later,
ground and granulated, sold as fertilizer.

She realizes the dead are dead
and begins to believe the truth:
like everyone else, she has spent her life
riding a sea-goat, tilting at windmills.
But today she dismounts from the damn
goat. Today she sees how her fingernails peel
and crack, how her hair grows and changes
color with age. Her nose smells the wild
daffodils, the campanula. She touches a scab
of bark on a beech tree, knows her limbs can
break like a stalk of wisteria, the small
leg of a bat. It is time to go home.
She thinks she will learn to make candles
and chocolate. Give these gifts to her mother.

If space is infinite, we are anywhere, at any point in space.
If time is infinite, we are at any point in time.

—JORGE LUIS BORGES

Cannon Splinter

Leda Burning, Immendorf Palace, 1945

—after Gustav Klimt's destroyed painting of Leda and the swan

the SS soldier
strikes his match on Leda's bare
back—the lecherous

swan's black neck
sinks into the curve
of her ass—the flesh

quivers as the fire
follows her spine to the nape,
to the hollow, fingers

blister as the gold leaf
in her hair curls into layers
of pitch-dark roses

and the painted bed
swirls in melted hues of green
before sucking Leda's last

breast into gray
ash, soot, and *sweet young*
thing sighs the soldier

Fortification

George, the man whose penis I sometimes hold,
has brought me to this old Austro-Hungarian spa town
surrounded by high mountain stone—a place
to hide from his battalion, the war, my spouse,
a place to look up from the valley
to the cliffs and imagine an army of husbands
running then suddenly stopped short.

Under the issued white terry-cloth cowl
I am Magdalena or the Madonna
and George is my Hieronymous or the bishop.
Together we move from fountain to fountain
clutching our blue ceramic cups:

the metallic water is thick and salinic
like ejaculate   in this water
we swim under marble ceilings
like manatees   we swim one-inch beyond extinction.

All but one café has been closed,
so the patients, the solitary doctor, the left-behind women
and Boris, the masseur who says he's too old to fight,
all of us   all eat together.

When George skips his shave, arrives at tea
with a dark-shadowed jaw, Boris complains
and sings propriety like my mother-in-law
hisses when her sons wear their hats to dinner.
But this was before her sons were old enough to march.

Before I learned to love the five o'clock shadow.
Before I knew George's face stubble   in concert with his tongue
licking my pink, licking my labia
gives me great pleasure. Who is Boris to deny pleasure?
Who is anyone to deny pleasure?

We soak in mud and nurse ourselves with minerals
and milk while on the other side of the mountain,
the bodies of a thousand men—husbands and fathers—
are cracking open.   Because we are sick
we can only drink our water and pretend not to hear.

A Crate of Oranges

sat next to the artist every afternoon

as he sipped tea on the café patio.
The people of Neulengbach assumed he traveled with citrus

because bright things must be a painter's constant companion.
Even when the war came and everyone succumbed

to wearing black
with a now-and-then splash of gun metal blue,

and the sound of the rock sparrow was replaced
by the wail of the young soldier's widow

as she watched the King's Guard, their posture spoiled
under the weight of oak and brass, load the coffin into the white
    carriage—

even then, the painter kept taking tea
with his box of happy, bulbous oranges,

so was credited with having a solid spirit.
But these people lived before modern art transformed a urinal,

before the time one could fly in a passenger jet, cruise the cloud-line
to see the earth for what it really is:

a patchwork of velvet: a brown, green, tourmaline grandmother's quilt,
soft and innocuous, smooth

except where the cities are.
By the end of the funeral, the widow's garter belt had slipped

causing her fishnet stocking to bunch at the right knee
of her long leg, reminding the painter of the cracked opal

in his mother's pendant.

By the end of the war
they had pulled the painter from his house,

burnt his blue sketches and paintings of naked girls, naked boys,
arrested him for using oranges as bait—

even though the village children swore the oranges were juicier
and sweeter than the ones placed in their stockings at Christmas

when the evergreen firs are hauled in from the cold
and the snow blinds all with a titanium white.

The Triumph of Light over Darkness, Vienna 1904

Shunned by the University for suggesting human existence consists of
nothing more than the infinitely repeated cycle of birth, copulation, and
death—Klimt guards his nearly finished mural with a shotgun, shouting
to his detractors from the balcony of the Great Hall:

"Is it my fault the jellyfish swamp the pier
in Binz, captivating the young couple
on their honeymoon?

Is it my fault the woman's legs dangle
over the edge of the dock as she questions
the motive behind cold Rügen air,
as she considers the sting of the jellyfish,
considers jumping into the chill-ice water
to grab, to hold the rubbery flesh in her fists?

Was I the one to put poison in the mandrake?
To pay the pugilist money for drawing blood?
There is little solace in this world
for those with swollen spleens—"

the painter pauses to add a stroke
of dark green under the waif's left breast—

"The couple will leave the jellyfish, go back
to the pink blankets of the boarding house,
caress each other into an assault of sweat
before collapsing on separate sides of the bed,
each the loneliest person in the world.

So off with your frog march, your machinery,
I guarantee your daughters will know
the right time to take off their clothes."

Ad Infinitum

The sex was never-ending
and beautiful like a billion poppies blowing
over the graves and empty houses
and the explosion in the distance

was beautiful like a billion poppies blowing
toward the east trying to escape the west
and the explosion in the distance
worked in our favor as you bent me over

toward the east trying to escape the west
and the pounding and the pounding
working in our favor as you bent me over:
like thunder and rain, a black blizzard, a charged sky

and the pounding and the pounding
like an orgasm to wake all neighboring armies:
like thunder and rain, a black blizzard, a charged sky
I heard myself coming until my throat was sore

like an orgasm to wake all neighboring armies
or the hard slap on a woman's round ass
I heard myself coming until my throat was sore
from screaming over the loud machines

or the hard slap on a woman's round ass
committed by a soldier on leave, a soldier gone AWOL
from screaming over the loud machines
saving his supply of butter and cinnamon for my nipples

suckled by a soldier on leave, a soldier gone AWOL
the one missing two fingers
licking his supply of butter and cinnamon from my nipples
because this is how we keep going

the one missing two fingers
pulling apart our clothes under the battle-broken sky
because this is how we keep going
like the atom eternally splitting

pulling apart our clothes under the century-long sky
the sex was never-ending
like the atom eternally splitting
over the graves and empty houses.

The Astrolabe

If I'd known how to interpret my grandmother's brass astrolabe,
    to register its dials and designs

    so to catch the warning

of this Ragnarök end
    of cruel winters between bed sheets—

would I have believed myself capable
of letting sea winds sift through my skirt
as I sought to send emails to a distant lover?

If I looked into the sky and saw the sleeping husband
    embedded in interplanetary positions—

the empty rooms, the crumbs—

would that have kept me from sneaking
    through city walls a year later? Kept me

from living between midnight and twilight?

o o o o

Turn the *rete* and *rule*, measure the angles, align the stars:

the astrologer predicts utopia and we nod our heads
    in disbelief, just as we did yesterday
        when she foresaw implosion.

We sail our fingers over a map of the South Pacific,
　　　　over the hollow skeleton of Tuvalo
　　　　　　and understand

　　　　　　　　we didn't save it

even when warned.

The stillmoon cavalier approaches
　　　　　　and, eyes closed, we grab
the lunar belly—

　　　　gallop away at the speed of crossed stars.

Baile Gitano

The flamenco dancer's thigh was pure lust
in the flood of night moon and I realized
I'd forgotten the splendor of lunar light
as your hand seized my arm, my body.
"Things must be forgotten—" you said,
in between bites of *paella*, rice cascading down
your chin. "Forget so you can enjoy again!
Experience comes only in the unexpected."

The waiter placed a wilted rose in my hair.
Red and yellow frogs—the size of my toes
and bright as the dancer's flaring skirt—
tapped round our chairs, our sandaled feet.
They glistened exotic, but the waiter said the frogs
were commonplace—a sign of the season's end
when the bay becomes a natural humidor: No good
for *baile*. Only the tobacco leaf thrives.
Bodies slip over each other, stick to bed sheets.

Undaunted, you moved closer. Your finger found
its home under the edge of my panties
as a crisp, pomegranate-filled *empanada* arrived
on my plate and I remembered to forget
as soon as the sweet red jelly touched my tongue.

It was easy enough to let the taste of jelly
and rum escape, but I knew abstracting men
from memory was never my method. I pressed
the blade of the guillotine, cutting you
another cigar, and the round head fell
without regret to the feet of frogs.

Reading Your Poems Translated from the Polish—

snow and origami swans

were almost enough
                    to keep me

from drinking
away another night. Almost

like the simple beagle waving her tail

is also almost enough,
                       but I still haven't seen

those rivers or glaciers or mothers
folding ribbons into flowers

that make it all something
                          better than the loud
                          braying of after-hours.

So I console myself
                    with one or two delusions:

we all suffer
             in our urge for more

& that someday:
      a thousand tea lights
           skinny girls in blue sandals
               a quilted canoe—

your baby in my belly,
kicking
humming away my selfish heart.

Bathtub Full of Gin

In upper Norway, the natives drink bathtub gin
during their dark prohibition winters of seam-
less ice. I, too, use the bathtub as sanctuary—
soaking in moonshine while I muse over my cracked
therapist who insists on lifting my skirt
until I scream that her couch is a battlefield,

a sexually bent, microfiber battlefield
where each session ends with limes dropped in gin
and tonic. But her clothes stay, always, so we can skirt
the issue of love and candle wax, or what seems
like love but may only be paprika on egg, cracked
and scrambled into the illusion of sanctuary,

similar to the illusion of *wild* in an animal sanctuary,
or the illusion that the victor on a battlefield
has conquered his foe, or won anything more than a cracked
spirit. Even so, I'd like to win this one—it'd help the gin
go down smoother if the thread in the seam
of her boots opened in fissures and her tight-lipped skirt

lifted in time to the rising of my own skirt—
but *ah!* My therapist insists on control. Her sanctuary
exists in the drenching of thighs in pure control: "Life seems
shitty," she scolds, "because it is. My battlefield
is full of pocked bones. Toes and nipples caught in the gin,
cut off clean. Wedding china always ends up cracked,

your mother, the sidewalk, this tooth—all cracked."
For her, the scandal of dropped glass is why a moat skirts
around the castle: "Fill the moat with Sapphire gin,
fill it with whatever it takes to keep the sanctuary,
to keep the precious-inside from the battlefield,
to keep what *is* separate from what only *seems*."

My therapist will never know the Self only seems
the jewel to protect. It's the Other who must never be cracked.
When she gets like this, I breathe away from the battlefield,
imagine mangos as flesh, a secret papaya under her skirt.
You may be wondering why I pay for this sanctuary-
building advice when I have my bathtub to sweat out the gin.

But trust is not a short skirt, it's a bowl of fruit and a battlefield.
Love is sweet berries of gin shooting from a cracked
cannon; it's the sanctuary of two bodies, the pain of welded seams.

Solitude

She comes hard in the window,
                  knowing sex heals before it destroys,
knowing the man pressing her against the glass
would have made a perfect lover for Frank O'Hara
who once said "I am the least difficult of men.
                      All I want is boundless love."

Afterward, she sits on the couch smoking French cigarettes—
forcing her asthmatic husband to lock himself in the back office—
and wonders why, most days, she can only have an orgasm
while dreaming of Angelina Jolie.

She pulls out the knife hiding under the cushion and scratches
the names of her future children into the coffee table.

Night and the noise of the blade couples
                      with the sound of beetles
beating their bodies against the window, desperate

for the other side.

Getting Your Work Before the World

Frank O'Hara's teeth looked like tombstones the second time
Alice Neel painted his face on canvas, capturing the freckles on his
  forehead.

It was because he was beat, she said. The lilacs in the background
were withered and Frank O'Hara was beat. The trouble came from love

of any kind. Alice knew this trouble like she knew what shade to paint
the down-turned look of the Haitian woman holding her dead child,

like she knew to blend her own grief in the color of stewed turnips
and to wear violet when listening to her shrink, a man who spent hours
  lecturing:

"many men in history have had mistresses, but I don't think any got
  paintings
as an extra bonus." And O'Hara himself knew there were never enough

words, never enough orange, always a lack of orange to complete the
  picture,
the image, the soda, the park, the half-dressed man. Not even enough

to add any citrus at all: no tangerines, no tangelos. Alice agreed
the man kissing the back of your neck was never the right one,

so she went to her married lover's apartment and claimed all that was
  hers,
all she'd given from inside. Hauled each canvas up the littered, yellow
  street.

The second time Frank O'Hara came to her door, discarded and unmet
by any man in the park, he looked beat, no longer the romantic falcon.

Alice painted him this way—sitting against a backdrop of dead lilacs,
his face a plague of indents, a factory of fatigue—to express his trouble,

to express the loss of what so many of us give and never remember to
collect.

Slumber-Dragon, Leap-Stallion: all brown earth in the end.
And the story of our lives just opens away—vacant, silent.

—Tu Fu

Dragon-Dance

Sometimes, the Trip Across the Continent is Enough

—for Deborah Digges, 1950-2009

A white dress waving in the wind—
           not a distress signal, something stronger
                is what I see when I picture you

                             floating

    among the empty seats of the university stadium.

Bare feet, long hair, dress all eyelets and gauze,
        lacking the restriction of buckles and buttons,

                          balancing

the height against the wind—
the student section, the press box, the nose bleeds.

A Botticelli gown
        waving to the lacrosse players
                practicing their pitch below. Not a distress signal,

something stronger: the full sail of the best pirate ship,
                        Queen Anne's Revenge.

ॐ

Because channeling your troubles into poetry
                              can only get you so far—

just like Lewis and Clark had to sometimes carry
            their boat through patches of prickly pear—

        the serious soul should never be land-locked.

Never have to carry the burden of three years'
            writing in a trunk on a pack-horse—the British
lurking behind every tree, Jefferson waiting
                              for his manuscript.

Sometimes, the trip across the continent is enough.
Six books, three husbands, enough.

        ❧

Heading back east, Lewis twice tried
                              to kill himself,
either by gunshot or jumping overboard.
            What if Lewis had stayed on the Oregon coast?

What if all poets lived seaside, beach-ready,
                              watching
the waves pull everything out past the lobster traps, the ship-men,
out and beyond the seam.

The plovers eat grubs and run the foam line.

                              Pour warm sand

over your legs
and the earth quiets.

                     Settled.

You no longer want to cut your hair short with a butcher knife
or color your naked body with Sharpie markers

                           and profanity.

ℳ

Two-hundred-years ago

                Mrs. Grinder, the keeper
of Grinder's Inn outside Nashville, found Lewis

                       with a razor,

cutting his flesh from head to toe. Bleeding
       from two bullet holes in his breast.

                      She slept

every night after, knowing his marred body
          was buried a few yards from her porch.

ℳ

But the mother of the lacrosse player who found your body
      outside the stadium
                is angry with you
for showing her daughter
the elasticity of the human form,
                     that the body

is just a body—warm liquid, wires and mesh, winters
of bone
         shining in the afternoon sun.

Everything else, everything but your body, whipped
      from the hem of your waving white dress   catching
        the most appropriate jet stream headed west.

Everything else flew over the Cold Spring Orchard, the apples
of Amherst—I'll tell the girl's mother

    you were half way across the continent

before you even hit the ground.

Memorial

The front page of the *Times* reports a new war
     memorial in Teaneck, New Jersey—

this and the honey
     on my morning toast

reminds me of you, my cousin, at ten-years-old,
surprised by the hive behind the loggers' cabin
hidden in the Sequoias,
               the giant trees named
for presidents and generals—

your mother, my mother, both afraid of bees,
snatched our small bodies away
                 before we could grab
our hoard of picnic candy, pine cones, and granite.

And now a room in New Jersey filled with long vertical chains
of joss paper squares:
               each bearing the name
     of a soldier killed in Iraq.

Made from bamboo or rice, parchment burned for the dead,
ghost money for Chinese ancestors to spend in the afterlife—

but in Teaneck, a memorial:
     4,000 squares of gold and silver foil
               set on white paper, a string of names—

You cried as we drove down the mountain road,
your face smeared with peanut butter and dirt.

Your face, the roadside bomb in Ramadi, a closed coffin.

A year later I'm still trying to imagine
        what could have been
                        in the pine box your wife clung to,
her garter slipping, her silk stocking bagged at the knee,

trying to imagine
        a faceless woman with a calligraphic pen,
writing the letters of your name, *Rowan*,

                        then sending them adrift
somewhere in the sunlit rooms of Teaneck.

U.S. Authorities Have About 14,000 Sets of Human Remains Lacking Identification

The last time I saw her she was leaving.
I tried to count the soft hairs on the nape
of her neck
as my boatman rowed her across the pond
away from my personal island.

There were no clouds that day.

We'd just finished lunch—
macaroni and cheese flavored with bacon—
and a conversation:

she'd made a remark about the beauty
found in Oslo's Vigeland Sculpture Park—
the arms and legs feeding
around the monolith,
the irony of 100 bodies
entwined and climbing to the top,
all carved from one giant block of granite.

I wanted her to mention my favorite stretch of the park:
the large naked women holding their large naked babies.

But she only said
it rained the day she went,
making it seem
as though the entire human condition had been crying.

I wanted her to have my baby.
She said no.
Either the world or her stomach was too full.

Claes and Renatta Spend Time Apart

When I visit a city, I eat as much as possible. I'm careful to live in variety: Never eat on the same corner twice. Talk to the city's people. Find out if they like their mayor. Read every newspaper. I make several sketches and count the number of dark-haired women. I decide what greatness the city may be lacking, and then I set out to make the city happy.

In London, I observed and I observed and it became obvious that everything comes in pairs. It seemed as though nothing could exist otherwise. That's why I wanted to give them a pair of knees. That's why I wanted to take Renatta with me, make her my half.

She told me New York needed love.

We crossed the ocean and the skyline tore into me. It wasn't like dark ogres dancing or gargoyles laughing. It was grey, not black, so it wasn't even death, just the square anatomy of a man. She told me night would be better, the lights should impress me. They didn't. To me, the lights remained a warning of what was to come.

So I ate and sketched and read. I counted the women. I made love to her every hour. Then the image of erect rabbit ears popped into my head. Pink, furry, and tall as the Empire State Building. I said aloud, "If two colossal bunny ears suddenly appeared in the Manhattan landscape, people would really look. What if you lived in Queens and, looking toward Central Park, you saw those ears? You might feel better about living in New York."

I felt I could operate on the world, bring her into me. Swedes believe in technology. Anything can be done. Anyone can be happy. I looked back at the island from the airport, at the structures stretching across Manhattan. There were no colossal rabbit ears, just the same pile of dark buildings. I could tell which window was hers by the order of the lights. She sat reading a book containing something stern, as all her books did. There were no bunny ears, but her brown hair fell down the back of the sofa, a beauty no man or city could memorialize.

Aphra Behn's Stocking

"...was in service to Charles II for only a year,"
I tell my mother, holding her attention long enough
for the nurse to drop a pill or two into her tea,
her fleeting mind a sucker for espionage and intrigue.

". . . then it retired to the wrist of the handsome
Dutch nobleman who loved Aphra—code name *Astrea*—
enough to whisper state secrets in her ear. She wrote
troop and ship movements in invisible. . ."

"He must have been a dolt," my mother cuts in,
"Only an idiot would bed down with a woman
from the opposition, then say too much—
and for what? A soiled sock?"

On my next visit, I return with a copy
of a portrait painted by a Flemish master,
a picture of a man who could've been Aphra's
aristocrat, upright in his cornflower blue suit.

My mother sees a sadness the color of pall bearers
in his eyes and I picture her chilled by the excitement
of the enemy's war plans divulged, seduced by the cloak,
the dagger, knotting her own nylon over his wrist.

"What kind of woman sells out her lover?"
she asks. I am
once again twelve years old

and my mother is riding her motorcycle
up to Hume Lake Camp
to pull me from the haze of dirt sweat and mosquitoes,

snapping me
from the dizziness of girls giggling
about boys, plotting over boys,
hiding
with boys in between the thick roots of trees

to tell me she's just told my father
about *him*,
the man she's loved
the last five years, their strange draped bodies

uncovered.

Message delivered, her muffler roars
back down
the curved mountain road:

leaving me to become the girl
at summer camp
whose mother rides a motorcycle.

Now, as my mother laments the Dutchman's fate,
I hear my father singing in the kitchen. He is still here.
They are still married. My mother wants to hear more
about Aphra Behn's underthings, her small stockinged feet.

I tell her Aphra did time in prison, and wrote "The Lover's
Watch," an argument on the art of making love in covert
corners and closets as unexpected as blue apples because
"Love ceases to be a pleasure when it ceases to be a secret."

And before she left her stocking in Antwerp,
she once visited Suriname. The colonial governor claimed
she hid her heart deep in the hollows of a Haida totem pole
that arrived aboard a returning slave ship.

My mother sighs as if to say she would've done the same thing.
And I remember, when I was eight, she told me she grew up
wanting to be a fireman, dreaming of climbing the tall ladder,
pulling smoke-stained children from windows in the sky.

Trees

—Oklahoma City, April 19, 1995

My grandfather once explained
how the seed of the giant Sequoia
is as small
and light as an oat flake,
only taking wind when flames have cleared the earth—

somehow he always finds me
in the midst of the great fires—

like the one outside my office window
breeding a ballet of falling ash, quiet dross
settling over debris, *a silence
already filled with noise.*

I can't hear anymore but see
how the firemen gathering broken children
turn into my grandfather
tying splints to new saplings,

and the broad-shouldered elm
shading the parked but burning cars
is my grandfather trimming the bamboo in his garden,

and the asphalt exploded, gashing the girth of its trunk:
the shrapnel scars lining his legs.

He would've loved this 80-year-old elm
in front of the hollowed out federal building,
half its limbs alight, for the same reason
he loved the Sequoias—the value of perennial beauty,

the way they stand patiently,
an army of monstrous Buddhas,
for a hundred years and then a hundred more—

the world is on fire
and all I can see is my grandfather's backyard,
his trees: the peach and orange, the nectarine he'd kept
for decades—tending its thin branches
despite its sterile belly, its lack of seed.

Tanglewood

Forever   I want to revel
in the kinetic clarity brought by real
            stars and trees and summer nights
                in Massachusetts,

blankets peopling the lawn at Tanglewood.

The exact night, our last night
four years ago when the sky put on
its nightshirt and Yo-Yo Ma's cello
            fondled the air, tickled the pines
                with the notes of Dvořák—

the heat of your hand, and the moment
            so much about the moment I never
                once thought about my dead father
or money owed, or how I used to own
            an ice chest named Roberta,

or my freshman year of college
spent masturbating in the library bathroom.

Maybe it's true that everyone's past
            sounds slightly better
when set to the music of a favorite rock epic,

            but if each existence comes down
                to birth, sex, and death,
                then I'll take the middle:

the hour before the ritual comes to completion,
                    the flash before

              the elder tribesmen knock
down the upright beams and the great log roof
          crashes upon the copulating couple.
          Whatever happens *before*

the dead bodies are pulled out, roasted and eaten.

Airlift

When Da Vinci made his drawings in Milan—
took up his black chalk to spin circles
around his aerial-screw—did he have my father
in mind? Five-hundred years later, barely
lifted up and away from the Mekong Delta
hot zone, two bullets in his thigh, clutching
the helicopter's metal skids with bare hands, body
hanging over paddy fields and swamplands
for the seven hour flight to safety.

               And my father?
Was his focus on slipping—or not slipping—
the scream in his knuckles, his leg,
the men left behind? On my mother,
the bank teller in Mendocino? Did he meditate
on the sugar-cane groves below, the cloudy
explosions, or the skein of waterways and canals?

Perhaps he thought simply of old man Da Vinci
(who knew how to build bombardments and cannons,
catapults and other war machines) sketching
the muscles of his Vitruvian man, trying to pin
down exactly where the human soul resides.
Though more than likely, my father managed
to hold tight just long enough by chanting over
and over,
       whirly-bird, whirly-bird, whirly-bird.

Our Brains are Built for This

So the wedding cake I smash
Into your face. So the male
spider dances and patterns his touch
to avoid becoming his lover's lunch.
So we say "I do" and paste ourselves
into albums. So the terrorist looks
both ways before crossing
the street, still whispering *inshallah*.
God willing each poet devises
her own death. Bottle. Bridge.
Broiler. We bury the dead in dark
wool and satin, say a prayer
before takeoff, and send
your mother a field of lilies
without concern of withering.
We flip through the pages and point
to the pictures of what we used
to look like. If I kiss your face
three times it means I love you.
So every Tuesday and Thursday
I order a *grande* iced mocha, one pump,
because our brains are built
for ritual. Because repetitive motion
moves material into something ethereal
for the dead to nosh on, so we go
to Home Depot and buy
a Christmas tree. Remembering
every time we bless ourselves, an angel
doesn't get his wings, but Cary Grant

lives on. And your asshole father?
My pushover mother? Some ornaments
have been in our family for years.

Peace and Happiness with Every Step

—her first husband drives her to the monastery—

The landscape changes and changes again
as we curve our way through chaparral
and dusted trailers, looking for heaven,

or at least the purest land we can find veiled
by this thick desert air. The rust on cars
and dirt on children reminds me I've failed

to keep myself clean. This is why we've come this far—
from the sea, through vineyards, to the inland rut
leading us past the poor dumb. We've driven my marred

self to the edge between waste and cliff, to this secret
village thrust in manzanita and oak woods.
There are monks hidden here, men and women shut

in with a fat bellied man. *Peace*: Kind words
drip off small scraps of colored papers tied to oak
tree arms. *Happiness*: inked onto rice-paper birds—

the words blow in the desert breeze. Mantras float
over my head. I wonder, do they ever grab
the paper leaves and eat them? Or are monastic throats

constantly content living among the lemonade-
berry sumac, their lonely bodies lying on canvas cots?
My husband brought me here to keep great

poets from seducing me, to keep my thoughts
grounded—mindful here, mindful now—to keep men
from treating me like Henry's Anne, her caught

head dropped like so many women brought to ruin.
For five days I am not to speak. I am to keep
meat from my mouth, my skin

covered in plain brown cotton. To bleed
the toxins from my brain. Buddhists from Viet Nam,
exiled, celibate. All mindful enough to teach

by example. One meal a day: calm,
quiet rice. Should I tell them my dad killed
his share of Viet Cong? They keep their heads drawn

over their bowls. They won't hear. Their minds are filled
with clean white grains. We meditate. We walk
with slow, concentrated steps. We are put to bed

when the sun falls. My ears strain under the night's smock:
to hear if they kiss when lights go out. My ears
reach hard: do monks snore? do they talk

in their sleep? The answer is lonesome and rears
into the moment I feared, but knew
would happen, if I could just be honest here

at Deer Park Monastery. It isn't due
to the blood I saw when my arm brushed
a prickly pear cactus this afternoon,

but more a result of monks chanting in hushed
tones. I wanted them to stop and sing Leonard
Cohen. I so desperately wanted them to crush

my heart with the song about Jane, the lock of hair,
the man who took the pain from her face,
the other man who couldn't save her.

Bells ring and these monks stop, bow, and embrace
Buddha. They don't do Leonard, but tell me to count
my breaths, as if numbering makes them mean less.

Under this dark Escondido sky, silence amounts
to my clothes coming off. I slip through my room,
through the door. A girl alive and wild in the village forest:

I weave naked through sharp branches. Under the half-moon,
I think the sounds of Sibelius and find peace.
The notes echo off meditation bongs, the bassoon

drifts over sleeping monks, and I can finally breathe.
My spirit hikes over the wooden cerise fence, I strike
my place, dig up my poet—we huddle in a corner, reading

love. I know the monastery won't miss me—religion, winglike,
can flutter through variations, a chameleon, making it so no one
need answer why some women prefer the binding warlike

arms of men, while others find happiness in solemn summer dusk.

Survival

The young man
who said honeybees are a dying breed
because our cell phone signals interfere with

the bees' buzzing lines of communication
was so ridiculously wrong—
and we were happy, already in the next

moment, lining the interstate, alert and apt
to swerve over a bridge kamikaze-style
to avoid any oncoming idiot.

Behind the wheel
the world seems like someone else's problem,
so we drive on

hoping it will be someone else's son,
someone else's country,
because every man wants to believe

our supply of honey bees is never-ending—
despite the parasitic mites moving
from hive to hive, sucking blood

from honey bee trachea. And who can blame us
for our faith? It's been decades since
the Manhattan Project, since the days

when rows of young girls
in freshly pleated skirts and printed blouses
sat atop stools in a Tennessee valley warehouse
separating uranium isotopes

                         with the slightest turn of the dial.

The Adulteress' Requiem for the Fall

The local woman with Tourette's is outside
        cursing our red brick building.
Someone has stirred her up

                  the way the tip of a finger
can tilt the stack of dishes just enough
        to stir the kitchen gnats who buzz
in the color of wounds.

        They've come in from the cold
and even the woman, in her thawed anger, knows

it's time to wear a wooly brown scarf, time to swear
        at the gods in search of covering.
                The leaves have turned,

then cracked. The jack-o-lanterns have spawned
        a hoary fungus over their eye-lids.

Even the late mallard has given up
        his mossy city pond, his icy water lilies.

And though I've buried my own
        indiscriminate season in the cold ground,
wrapped my breasts in a Siberian winter shawl
        to bid *adieu adieu,*

the little girl inside is still laughing,
still curling her R's to say: *rescue, rivulet, résumé*—

always happy under the suffocating sweat
  of her plastic vampire mask.

The First Husband Buried

After eight years of empty threats,
all I can do is watch him study the high
lamp over our bed, his mind knitting
a noose from ties he never wore. He tells
me he's never been good at anything.
He tells me he's sorry he has to leave.
I start to give my opinion on the mode
at which he will arrive at death.
I tell him the ceiling fan isn't strong enough
to hold his weight. He begins a fad diet.
I tell him a widow who finds her husband
in dead sleep will fare better than the one
who finds her spouse's brain scattered
about the room, slivers of skull cleaving
to their wedding photo. I suggest pills, but
he says poison lacks drama, so I put
in a motion for a public performance,
a place where someone else will find his corpse.
If you must, I tell him, you must.
I start to see myself single.
I learn French. I run for office.
I adopt children from Madagascar.
I bury every minute of every day. I do
this because I must. Because the cliché
about the sinking ship carries more heft
than the fact no one will be here to trim
the branches from the front tree. Let its arms
grow, grope their way over the window
to stave off the intruder, the sun.

"Time is Forever Dividing Itself Toward Innumerable Futures
and in One of Them I am Your Enemy."

—Jorge Luis Borges

Before I stopped dreaming about Todd and his great
lifeguard tower, his hands and my bikini;
before you stopped scheming about Mary Kate's

small wrists and the time you touched her bare knee;
before Sean married Maureen, and Dan sold
his house for a ship with two sails—we

were all friends. Summers we sucked ice-cold
vodka from watermelon, grilled fish, and watched
the sun dip below the sea. At Christmas, we wore ribald

holiday sweaters, drank ourselves into debauchery,
smashed ornaments on our heads, the walls,
then tip-toed naked over the shards, played hopscotch.

We had jobs but no bawling
children. My husband, remember the waves
and the small plovers weaving between our bodies?

We were infinite for a time. Until the houses
began to fall into the sea and your brother was killed
in the right-turn lane of the Pacific Coast Highway.

The Swedish nanny broke Dan's heart, and we'd all slapped
each other too many times. Now I am not your friend.
I never think of you as I sit in the thick reeds

of another country, posing in another photo's caption,
some other man's wife—I paint turnpikes and sugarcane
on my ankles. We've successfully wrapped

ourselves in different Christmas parties, different planes
of existence, and in all of them, you walk straight
despite the headwind, hot in your blue raincoat.

But in one of them, I am your friend. I wait
and wipe the water from your face before moving
into the softer fabric of a warmer man's climate,

I lift your head and hold your ear to the shark-eye
shell resounding laughter over the turbulent waves.

Jesus Wet the Bed Like You

So your father interrupted your mother's plan
to become a dowager
when he sold the house in secret,
gathered his bones and nails and sailed
out of town via the drawbridge exit.

The stress of relocations fell onto your mother's brow—
seaport to seaport, aunt to uncle—
and she was forced to battle
your sudden insecurity with a rubber bed sheet
and a sweet singing budgerigar.

You named the bird after your father
and never once thought
about how your mother felt
when the signalman's light pointed
from the lighthouse, flooding her bedroom window.

Now, at your father's funeral, I'm watching you
stand clear-eyed and angry, peeling
the shell of an orange (as you must) to reach the pulp,
and the proper time has come
to think of all the good that can come from an enema,

from quarantine,
from the shifting nature of gloom—
so the next time it hurts, remember,
my warm hand will be there
to cradle your sad but handsome testicles.

The Locusts Are Swarming

I passed through the wild market streets unharmed
   until the West African woman
stopped me with her eyes and kept me with the color
   of her dress, the color of the dropped sun.

Then she called to my lips, my torn insides:
   "Let him in for the night, *amie*.
Now the locusts are swarming through *Cote d'Ivoire*,
   flying through villages like paper birds.
The children are jumping through bright yellow wings
   and the other world is stirring for love."

She clicked her tongue and motioned to the table at her waist
   full of small wooden men, wooden women.
"*Quatre dollars*. It's your *blolo bian*, your other world lover.
   He's angry with you. Let him in.
Quatre dollars s'il vous plait. Let him in for the night
   or the pain will never leave your stomach,
      the seams of your house will continue to rip."

She shoved a wooden man into the palm of my hand.
   I touched the smooth of his jacaranda body,
   his slender limbs and painted ocean eyes.

"He is yours, you know, *petite fille*. The man who eats
   your food and sleeps in your bed is for earth.
But this one's the one from before you were born.
   He stomps through your mind, *sans cesse*
   —because you are his.

The locusts are swarming and women come crying
   but the Baule people know to take this man,
   the one in your hand, and let him in."

I touched the smooth of his jacaranda body and listened
   to the woman from *Cote d'Ivoire* tell me
why the pit of my stomach bleeds, why the front step
   stays loose, why the faucet still leaks,
why the shape of everything keeps falling flat:
   All men and women have two lovers.
The one that isn't here can never be left empty.

Not wanting things to rip further,
   I gave her four dollars.
   And you I let in.

Scenes from the Explorer's Second Wedding

—to the one left behind

As the pig turned on the spit, its jealous pineapple eyes
    watched the beads of my bridal gown shimmer,
watched me every half-rotation—half saw me wet
    my ashen lips, half saw the groom lick
    pork juice from my wrist—

and I was reminded of Rosemary and Guy snorting lines
    of cocaine in their red room over the red bar in New Orleans,
of how afraid you were to sniff the line down Rosemary's arm!
    of how Rosemary and Guy dreamed they'd marry
    and live in Hawaii one day, a happy story, a love story.

But this was *my* wedding, the last time I'd look to the past—
    the future all smoked mullet, all flesh, all Florida sunshine.

Then my groom dipped his silver cup in the wedding fountain,
    its water like the sapphire water of Lake Louise,
    and the memory of five-hundred Japanese tourists
rose from the depths of Alberta's glacial tarns.
    And you! their captain hot at the helm,
dictating a curse on my future: a litany of swamplands,
    mosquitoes and hurricanes, palmetto bugs
    and horned gators. So once again,

I fought back. The human vessel can only hold so much
    beauty, so I turned away from this legion of the past:

I'm no longer sipping whiskey and water in awe of Helena's
 one big mountain, begging you to be happy and graceful.
 There's no room left for Europe's dead,
for the Italian cemetery full of Kiwi cadets and red roses.
 I'm walking the aisle now. *Non, je ne regrette rien.*
But *ah!* how the music always stops.

And there is no reprieve, I learn this: We can never leave
 the worlds we once inhabited. In the audience
 my uncle's smoldering cigar grabs my thoughts and there
you are in cotton broadcloth, smoking a tiny cigarillo
 somewhere in the Keys—a looming specter bat.

Notes

In "Seven Things She Learned Along the Way," the line "The attraction of the glass is balanced by the contrary attraction of the liquor" is from Sir Isaac Newton's *Opticks* (1704); and the line "So many things balance the sorrow of it" is from Joseph Butler's *Human Nature and Other Sermons* (1887).

The Frank O'Hara quote in "Solitude" is from O'Hara's poem "Meditations in an Emergency" (1957).

The title of "U.S. Authorities Have About 14,000 Sets of Human Remains Lacking Identification" is taken from the title of a USA Today cover story on June 25, 2007.

The fictional speaker in "Claes and Renatta Spend Time Apart" is inspired by the artist Claes Oldenburg. The quoted passage is from Oldenburg's *Proposals for Monuments and Buildings*, 1965-69 (1969).

In "Trees," the line "a silence already filled with noise" is from John Ashbery's poem "Some Trees" (1956). The word 'noise' is plural in Ashbery's poem.

Acknowledgments

Grateful acknowledgment is made to the editors of the following journals where poems included in *Latest Volcano* first appeared:

Alehouse: "Bathtub Full of Gin"
Beloit Poetry Journal: "Ad Infinitum" and "Fortification"
Briar Cliff Review: "*Baile Gitano*"
Connotation Press: "Airlift"
The Chattahoochee Review: "Getting Your Work Before the World"
Cutthroat: "A Crate of Oranges"
Fugue: "Peace and Happiness with Every Step," "She Took the Gun," and "Tanglewood"
The Gettysburg Review: "Time is forever dividing itself toward innumerable futures and in one of them I am your enemy." and "The First Husband Buried"
The Greensboro Review: "Scenes from the Explorer's Second Wedding"
Harpur Palate: "Horse-Driven Men"
Mead: The Magazine of Literature and Libations: "Survival"
Meridian: "Trees" and "Memorial"
The North American Review: "The Locusts Are Swarming" and "Our Brains Are Built for This"

The Portland Review: "The Adultress' Requiem for the Fall," "Reading Your Poems Translated from the Polish," "The Triumph of Light over Darkness, Vienna 1904," and "U.S. Authorities Have About 14,000 Sets of Human Remains Lacking Identification"
Prairie Schooner: "Nothing to See Here" and "What Remains"
Puerto del Sol: "Aphra Behn's Stocking"
Rhino: "Claes and Renatta Spend Time Apart"
Tampa Review: "*Leda* Burning, Immendorf Palace, 1945"

"Sometimes, The Trip Across the Continent is Enough" was selected for *Best New Poets 2009: 50 Poems from Emerging Writers*, edited by Kim Addonizio and Jeb Livingood.

"Nothing to See Here" also appeared in the anthology *Women Write Resistance: Poets Resist Gender Violence*, edited by Laura Madeline Wiseman.

꙳

Thanks to my family: Moose, Nanny, Poppy, Mary, Ethan, and my bestie Laura Cheek. I would not have come this far without your love and encouragement. And to my early mentors for their care and guidance: Victoria Featherstone, Glover Davis, and Sandra Alcosser.

I am indebted to Stephanie Strickland for choosing my manuscript for the 2015 Marsh Hawk Press Poetry Prize, and to Jon Curley for his keen editing eye.

Special thanks to my awesome friends Kara Candito and Erin Belieu for their help shaping this manuscript through its various stages.

And most of all, I am eternally grateful to Timothy Daniel Welch, my life partner, my best man, my love's collaborator, for the time and generosity devoted to this book and its author.

About the Author

TANA JEAN WELCH earned her MFA in Poetry from San Diego State University and her PhD in English from Florida State University. Her poems have appeared in journals including *The Southern Review*, *The Gettysburg Review*, *Beloit Poetry Journal*, *Prairie Schooner*, and the anthology *Best New Poets*. Born and raised in Fresno, California, she currently teaches literature and writing at the Florida State University College of Medicine.

TITLES FROM MARSH HAWK PRESS

Jane Augustine, *KRAZY: Visual Poems and Performance Scripts, A Woman's Guide to Mountain Climbing, Night Lights, Arbor Vitae*

Thomas Beckett, ~~*DIPSTICK*~~ *(DIPTYCH)*

Sigman Byrd, *Under the Wanderer's Star*

Patricia Carlin, *Quantum Jitters, Original Green*

Claudia Carlson, *Pocket Park, The Elephant House*

Meredith Cole, *Miniatures*

Jon Curley, *Hybrid Moments*

Neil de la Flor, *An Elephant's Memory of Blizzards, Almost Dorothy*

Chard deNiord, *Sharp Golden Thorn*

Sharon Dolin, *Serious Pink*

Steve Fellner, *The Weary World Rejoices, Blind Date with Cavafy*

Thomas Fink, *Joyride, Peace Conference, Clarity and Other Poems, After Taxes, Gossip: A Book of Poems*

Norman Finkelstein, *Inside the Ghost Factory, Passing Over*

Edward Foster, *Dire Straits, The Beginning of Sorrows, What He Ought To Know, Mahrem: Things Men Should Do for Men*

Paolo Javier, *The Feeling Is Actual*

Burt Kimmelman, *Somehow*

Burt Kimmelman and Fred Caruso, *The Pond at Cape May Point*

Basil King, *The Spoken Word/the Painted Hand from Learning to Draw/A History 77 Beasts: Basil King's Bestiary, Mirage*

Martha King, *Imperfect Fit*

Phillip Lopate, *At the End of the Day: Selected Poems and An Introductory Essay*

Mary Mackey, *Travelers With No Ticket Home, Sugar Zone, Breaking the Fever*

Jason McCall, *Dear Hero,*

Sandy McIntosh, *Cemetery Chess: Selected and New Poems, Ernesta, in the Style of the Flamenco, Forty-Nine Guaranteed Ways to Escape Death, The After-Death History of My Mother, Between Earth and Sky*

Stephen Paul Miller, *There's Only One God and You're Not It, Fort Dad, The Bee Flies in May, Skinny Eighth Avenue, Any Lie You Tell Will Be the Truth*

Daniel Morris, *If Not for the Courage, Bryce Passage, Hit Play*

Sharon Olinka, *The Good City*

Christina Olivares, *No Map of the Earth Includes Stars*

Justin Petropoulos, *Eminent Domain*

Paul Pines, *Divine Madness, Last Call at the Tin Palace, Charlotte Songs*

Jacquelyn Pope, *Watermark*

George Quasha, *Things Done For Themselves*

Karin Randolph, *Either She Was*

Rochelle Ratner, *Ben Casey Days, Balancing Acts, House and Home*

Michael Rerick, *In Ways Impossible to Fold*

Corrine Robins, *Facing It: New and Selected Poems, Today's Menu, One Thousand Years*

Eileen R. Tabios, *Sun Stigmata, The Thorn Rosary: Selected Prose Poems and New (1998–2010), The Light Sang As It Left Your Eyes: Our Autobiography, I Take Thee, English, for My Beloved, Reproductions of the Empty Flagpole*

Eileen R. Tabios and j/j hastain, *the relational elations of ORPHANED ALGEBRA*

Susan Terris, *Ghost of Yesterday, Natural Defenses*

Madeline Tiger, *Birds of Sorrow and Joy*

Tana Jean Welch, *Latest Volcano*

Harriet Zinnes, *New and Selected Poems, Weather Is Whether, Light Light or the Curvature of the Earth, Whither Nonstopping, Drawing on the Wall*

YEAR	AUTHOR	MHP POETRY PRIZE TITLE	JUDGE
2004	Jacquelyn Pope	*Watermark*	Marie Ponsot
2005	Sigman Byrd	*Under the Wanderer's Star*	Gerald Stern
2006	Steve Fellner	*Blind Date With Cavafy*	Denise Duhamel
2007	Karin Randolph	*Either She Was*	David Shapiro
2008	Michael Rerick	*In Ways Impossible to Fold*	Thylias Moss
2009	Neil de la Flor	*Almost Dorothy*	Forrest Gander
2010	Justin Petropoulos	*Eminent Domain*	Anne Waldman
2011	Meredith Cole	*Miniatures*	Alicia Ostriker
2012	Jason McCall	*Dear Hero,*	Cornelius Eady
2013	Tom Beckett	~~*DIPSTICK*~~ *(DIPTYCH)*	Charles Bernstein
2014	Christina Olivares	*No Map of the Earth Includes Stars*	Brenda Hillman
2015	Tana Jean Welch	*Latest Volcano*	Stephanie Strickland

For more information, please go to: **www.marshhawkpress.org**